KiKi!

So So!

Oink Oink!

[illegible]

2012

Pigs Over Shambhala

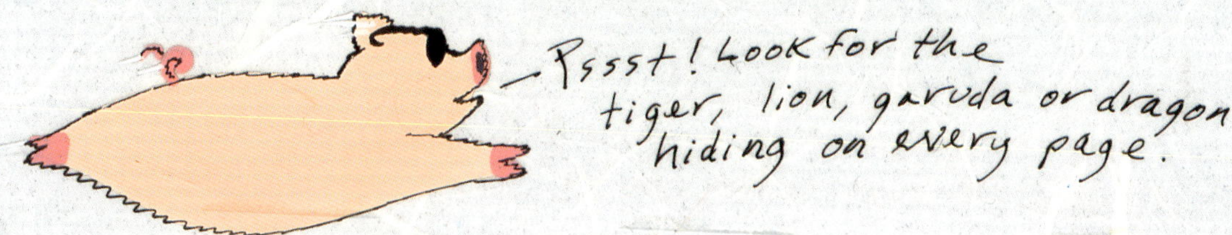

Dear Readers,

These ABC rhymes are designed to foster pride in our Shambhala world and to provoke interesting conversations about Shambhalian Buddhist principles. Older children will understand the commentary, younger children will enjoy the ABCs and playful rhythm and rhyme, toddlers will be content to follow the flying sky-piggy and adults will enjoy the whole thing as a light-hearted satire. The hidden animals should be fun for everyone!

Kerry Lee MacLean, Infinite Lotus of Dharma

On the SPOT!
BOOKS

Pigs Over Shambhala

An ABC for Young Warriors of All Ages.

Written and Illustrated by Kerry Lee MacLean

A is for Shambhala ARTS

The warriors of Shambhala practice arts every day.
To dance or ride or golf with grace, that's the warrior's way.

Any art form or sport can be used to wake ourselves up, if it's done mindfully. We can draw pictures, make music, sing, dance, march, ride horses and even golf, all as meditative actions.

Hidden Animal: Tiger

B is for BRAVE and Perky Lion

Like the brave and perky snow lion we're cheerful even when we're camped out in the mountains and it starts to rain again.

The strength of Snow Lion isn't about pretending to be happy when we're not. It's about keeping a brave and cheerful attitude, even when life isn't going our way. Snow Lion is the Shambhala warrior's second strength or dignity.

Hidden Animal: Garuda

C is for CALLIGRAPHY

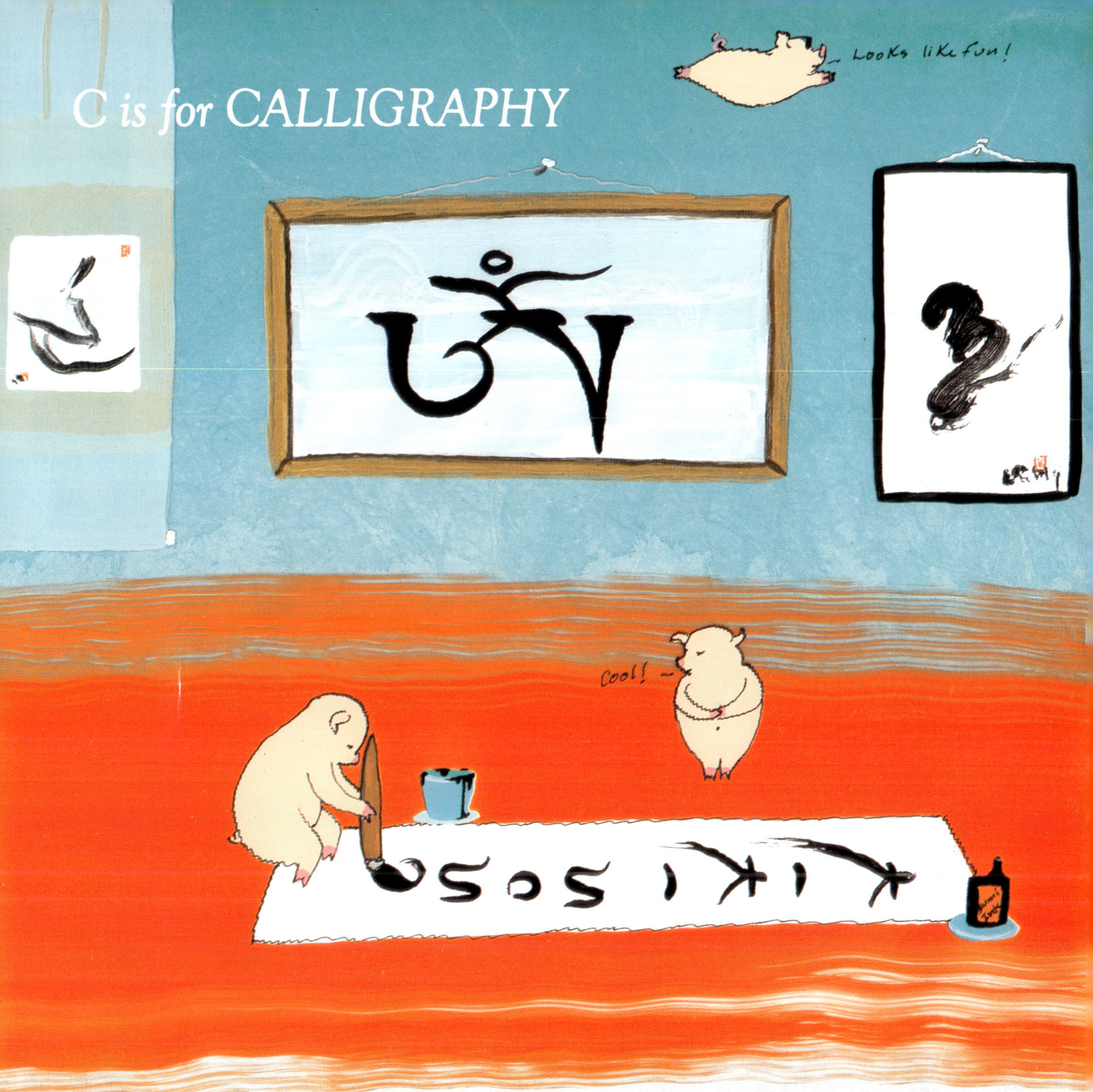

When you do calligraphy you're not supposed to think.
Let go, let go, let go and feel the flowing of the ink!

Of course, you start out with some idea of what you want to paint, but then you let go of your thoughts and just watch the ink flow onto the blank paper, as it will.

Hidden Animal: Snow Lion

D is for DRALA

When you're out for a walk, be awake, be aware.
The magic of the dralas is everywhere!

Dralas are the power and magic that exist in our natural world. If we respect them, they'll stay around and maybe even help us. If we disrespect them, they'll go away, leaving our world feeling kind of like an empty shell.

Hidden Animal: Garuda

E is for EIGHT Year Olds' Rites of Passage

At the tender age of eight, we learn the warrior's bow,
then being kind to *everyone* becomes our lifelong vow.

At eight children are old enough to take the vow of kindness. Also, they are old enough to be a real help to their families. In Rites class kids learn to practice the Shambhala arts and to meditate with their friends.

Hidden Animal: Dragon

F is for FLOWER Arranging

A heaven branch comes down to earth with blessings from above,
then man joins it all together with a flower, which is love.

Ikebana teaches us to create harmony in the chaos of our world. The heaven branch is the tall one, the earth leaves cover the ground and man, or human, is the flower, joining heaven and earth together with our tender heart.

Hidden Animal: Tiger

G is for GREAT Eastern Sun

If you want to live a life filled with friendships, peace and fun,
you've got to see the goodness shining out from everyone.

The Great Eastern Sun shows our goodness always rising up out of every situation, just like the sun rises up out of the darkness every morning.

Hidden Animal: Tiger

H is for HALIFAX

Come sailing in to Halifax, Shambhala's royal seat,
then visit Dorje Denma Ling for Sun Camp or retreat.

Halifax is a harbor city in Nova Scotia and Dorje Denma Ling is a place in the country outside Halifax where the magic of Sun Camp and all kinds of meditation programs takes place.

Hidden Animal: Garuda

I is for INSCRUTABLE Dragon

The dragon never shows people the place where he resides,
we just hear his rolling thunder from the great sky where he hides.

The Dragon helps everyone he meets in his own mysterious way and although he's all powerful, he is kind to even the smallest creatures. Dragon is the fourth strength or dignity of the Shambhala warrior.

Hidden Animal: Garuda

J is for JOKES and Laughter

In Shambhala jokes and laughter can be heard throughout the day.
Our hearts and minds stay healthy when we lighten up and play.

We try not to take things TOO seriously. It's important to keep a good sense of humor so that we can always delight in our world.

Hidden Animal: Tiger

K is for Shambhala KING

When the all-good Sakyong King joins heaven and earth,
we feel the rising of the sun and our hearts give birth.

The Sakyong King is our enlightened leader. He teaches us how to meditate and helps us become the very best people we can possibly be.

Hidden Animal: Dragon

L is for LOVING Kindness

Since they may have been your mother in another long-past time,
treat each one you meet with kindness, it will make you feel sublime.

Since all people, animals and insects are born over and over and over again, anyone you meet could have been your mother in another life! So, we owe it to all beings to be friendly and respectful.

Hidden Animal: Dragon

M is for MEDITATION

When your wild mind is filled with fear and hesitation,
peace and confidence will come from sitting meditation.

Sitting meditation is hard to do, so why does everyone do it? Because it calms our anger and our fears. Our minds become peaceful, clear, happy and strong.

Hidden Animal: Tiger

N is for NAROPA University

Naropa is the coolest school, all warriors agree,
to learn to paint and sing and think and write good poetry.

Naropa is a Buddhist college in Boulder, Colorado. They teach meditation, painting, writing, dancing and the many different ways of helping others. Naropa was started by our great friend and first teacher, Chogyam Trungpa, Rinpoche.

Hidden Animal: Snow Lion

O is for OUTRAGEOUS Garuda

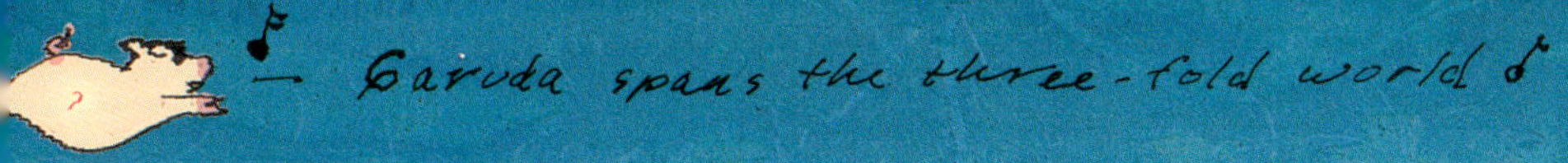

Cracking from a turquoise egg the red garuda hatches,
and flaming like the phoenix bird, she rises from her ashes.

Sometimes in life it's wise to be completely outrageous. Garuda shows us how. Garuda is the warriors' third strength, or dignity.

Hidden Animal: Garuda

P is for PRINCE Siddhartha

Prince Siddhartha gave it all away to sit beneath a tree.
He said that he would not get up until his mind was free.

Wealthy Prince Siddhartha suddenly realized all his riches couldn't bring him long lasting happiness, so he left his palace and started meditating under a tree. Finally, he felt clear-headed and his heart was filled with joy. People started calling him Buddha, which means 'one who is awake'. Then he taught all of them how to meditate, too.

Hidden Animal: Dragon

Q is for Shambhala QUEEN

Our queen, the Sakyong Wangmo, harvests peace just like the song.
We see by her example to be cheerful, kind and strong.

The Sakyong Wangmo is Shambhala's queen. She works to keep peace and harmony in the land.

Hidden Animal: Tiger

R is for ROCKY Mountain Shambhala Center

As we arrive and smell the pinetrees, the first thing that we see
is the sight of the stupa shining out so splendidly!

The Great Stupa of Dharmakaya is at Rocky Mountain Shambhala Center. The stupa is the heart and mind of our first Sakyong shining out. His name was Chogyam Trungpa, Rinpoche, and he brought the Shambhala teachings to us all the way from Tibet.

Hidden Animal: Snow Lion

S is for SUN Camp

We sing tiger, lion, garuda, dragon all day long,
and discover basic goodness as we march on and on.

Sun Camp is the summer training ground for young warriors, ages ten through sixteen. The basic goodness we discover is the goodness that lives inside every living thing and every human being without exception.

Hidden Animal: Garuda

T is for TIGER's Meekness

Like the tiger we tread softly across the forest floor.
We don't brag about ourselves and start acting like a bore.

The tiger doesn't need to brag, show off or put others down to build himself up because he's already so sleek and powerful, and because he has a humble, tender heart.

Hidden Animal: Dragon

U is for UNDERSTANDING

Buddha, Christ and Dr. King shared wisdom we can use:
Think twice before you judge someone, walk miles in their shoes.

When everyone on this earth can see things from each others point of view, for the first time in history we will have world peace.

Hidden Animal: Tiger

V is for VICTORY Over War

Most barbarian battles bring great misery and more,
but, Shambhala skirmishing leads to victory over war.

During skirmishing we learn how to be true warriors who are mindful, even in conflict. We learn to be dignified leaders and to care for our people. That is the description of a Shambhala warrior. You might know someone at home or at school who <u>*you*</u> *think is a Shambhala warrior.*

Hidden Animal: Tiger

W is for WINDHORSE

When you're depressed and confused and you don't know what to do,
bring your energy together and ride your windhorse through!

To ride windhorse means to gather together your inner strength and goodness and ride it like a great wind to uplift yourself.

Hidden Animal: Dragon

X is for X Marks-the-Spot

X marks the spot in Europe where young people want to be.
Dechen Choling is the place kids go to set their big minds free.

Dechen Choling is our meditation center in the gentle countryside of France. People, young and old, come here from all over Europe to practice together.

Hidden Animal: Garuda

Y is for YUMI and YA

With your yumi and your ya, you cut through hope and fear.
But, kyudo's NOT a sport! It's to keep you calm and clear.

The yumi is the samurai warrior's bow and the ya is the arrow. We shoot the same way people have in Japan for hundreds and hundreds of years, not as a sport, but as a moving meditation.

Hidden Animal: Snow Lion

Z is for ZIJI (Confidence)

Ziji is the confidence that comes from being real.
Take pride in who you are and show others how you feel.

Even if you're having a rotten day, it's important to take pride in who you are and to realize that you do belong here, there is a place for you in this world.

Hidden Animal: Dragon

Aurevoir!
The End.

My greatest appreciation and thanks to my dear friend, the very kind and generous Marie-Luise Walter-Elliott. You are the BEST!

And special thanks to those who kindly took the time to offer insight and encouragement: Acarya Judith Simmer-Brown, David Brown, Mark Thorpe, James Elliott, Kelly MacLean, Andrew MacLean, Sophie Maclaren, Tessa Maclaren, Kevin Hoagland, Amy Nicolson-Kida, Emily Takahashi, Tania Leontov, the outlaw Tracey Outlaw, Alexandra Shenpen, Norah (Queen Norah) Murray and, of course, my all-good and loving husband, Hector Hector MacLean, III.

Published by On the Spot! Books
Phone/Fax 303-666-0550
1492 Tipperary Street
Boulder, CO 80303
USA

Printed in Hong Kong, ISBN 0-9652998-3-X

Distributed by Ingram Book Company, Books West (303) 449-5995
and On the Spot! Books (303) 666-0550

Other picture books available from
On the Spot! Books:

Boulder People's Choice Award Winner
PIGS OVER BOULDER
also
PIGS OVER DENVER
PIGS OVER COLORADO
and SOPHIE'S NOT AFRAID!

To order call 303-666-0550